For Mary Louise Arnold
con affetto —

Ralph de Toledano

10/1/96

The Apocrypha
of Limbo

The Apocrypha of Limbo

Ralph de Toledano

PELICAN PUBLISHING COMPANY
Gretna 1994

*The word "Pelican" and the depiction of a pelican
are trademarks of Pelican Publishing Company, Inc., and
are registered in the U.S. Patent and Trademark Office.*

Library of Congress Cataloging-in-Publication Data
Toledano, Ralph de, 1916-
    The apocrypha of limbo / Ralph de Toledano.
      p. cm.
    ISBN 1-56554-066-2
    I. Title.
    PS3554.E85A87 1994
    811'.54—dc20   94-6559
                                        CIP

"Three Devotions" was first published in *Modern Age;* "Epilogue to
the Book of Job" in *Commentary;* "David Antiphons" in *American
Scholar;* "Prologue to the Book of Jesse" in *The Standard;* "Until That
Time" in *Triumph;* "Letter from the City" and "Cocktail Hour" in
Hillsdale Review; "After Pliny" in *Yale Literary Magazine;* and "Muerte
del Poeta" in *La Garrita* in Puerto Rico.

Manufactured in the United States of America

Published by Pelican Publishing Company, Inc.
1101 Monroe Street, Gretna, Louisiana 70053

For my wife,
Eunice

non mihi—no tibi—sed nobis

The Apocrypha of Limbo

THREE DEVOTIONS

Entreme donde no supe
y quedeme no sabiendo

S. Juan de la Cruz

Go to the thicket:
in the hollow tree
a face is hidden, its mouth
bloody as a pomegranate.

The thicket and the tree
mean nothing,
but in the face lurks more
than the secret eyes.

Lift up the face:
there is no bone behind it,
only the terrible accoutrement of shape
depthless as water.

I.
Who seeks God's love seeks nothing.
Against the measurable span
of finite longing, hope delimited,
God's love is less and more than love,
not to be given or withheld
but there in the eternal abyss
of all creation. Who seeks
in life more than the benediction
of God's presence, lacking love
or hate or anything but the Presence,
covets a hurricane in a thimble.

Love is an interchange, a giving
and a receiving, in the tiny night
a touching of equal fingers, a hale
for the all too sudden flesh.
But who knows God to love Him, who
has seen through tear-flushed eyes
the monster Amplitude. Not man.
Not the ineffective body,
the trembling soul clutching
the edge of earth and heaven.

Who seeks God's love seeks nothing
but the cold reflection in a pool.
Who offers God his love presents
a microbe to behemoth.
There is no giving, no receiving,
only the timeless instant when
the panting beast touches tongue to water,
the complex silence when the heart
turns outward from despair and blasphemy,
hearing the single syllable of God's will.

II.
The final phrase is not progenitive;
it is the final phase.
The final gasp is not the first
utterance but matter gagging on eternity.
For there is no beginning that is not
an ending, but no ending is a beginning.
In the final moment, it is all done
and not to be undone, all said
never to be unsaid, caught in rock.

The final phrase is the beginning word
and not the final silence.
The final gasp is not the final cry
but the tentative rehearsal
of the unmeasured song, for each end
is the beginning of a greater end.
In the final moment, there is no death
regurgitative but the final birth.

In not dying there is death,
and in not being there is life.
At the end of time, time is endless.
In the moment of rejection there is acceptance,
and in complete desire complete negation.
In logic there is chaos and in chaos order.
In the final moment, all is
meaningless but the one meaning.

III.
In these, my private devotions
there are no roads, no signs,
no thin horizon smudged by use or time,
only a skeleton to rattle in the light,
and the taste of salt on my lips,
and the honk and hoot of my desires.
In the private moment that is all.

Who then can speak to God?
The tangible nail in the vanished skin?
Who knows the syllables of recompense,
the torpid epithet,
the burbling sigh and gasp?

The single mind returns to its single
station, but the noise of stone is no
hallelujah to the God within.
The silence of the variable pulse
gauges the irremedial span.
The visible hope divides
the gesture at the door,
the tender murder at the gate of Hell.

In these my private devotions
there is only the adequacy of not enough,
as when the mind returns
to the overt scrutiny of the public square.

DAVID ANTIPHONS

O Sapientia, O Adonai, O Radix Jesse

The Seven Os of Advent

he will whet his sword

In the muted wood,
I walked alone
till screaming angels
moved like a knife
across my eyes.

Lord, in the huts
and in the mud your angels
screamed to the heavens
and the sheltered wood
was quiet no longer.

In the night I waited
torn in my sleep
seeing the sky unfolded,
feeling the earth unhinged:
and then I knew, my Lord,
and then I knew.

hold not thy peace at my tears

Untouched among the winds
you came, making the night holy.

No hands to greet you, no bursting
shout to make a mark on time,
no glory to misspeak your name.

Gravely among the men who courted death
you sat, meek to their clamor, cool
to their plighted arrogance.

But in your hand, the seed opened,
and in the rending noise and terror
silence was everywhere.

bow down thine ear

Turn to me in the night, Lord,
mouth twisted in irony and pain.
Seek me out in the night,
unhallowed in the flesh.

Strike me with gladness, Lord,
and unforgiveness, stiff-necked.

Break out the stars, my Lord,
and sing or wail:
let penitents cluster.

under his tongue is mischief

Into what riveted cycle,
Lord, have we been thrust,
groaning at the blistered nerve?

What is the new concrescence
which writhes in naughty purpose?
And is this sudden night, O Lord,
a casual pit or a Cartesian well?

Briefly in spring the awkward pattern
urges a passion and subsides;
briefly the burgeoning excellence
gutters in the backwash of days.

So when the tropic echo wanes,
when the heart is cold again,
old birds a-croak defile renewal.
Then is it done, my Lord, all done?

with a double heart

Where will the strength be found
for morning's work
and then at evening's end
the power to pray?

Where will I find the hand
of benison, in priestly
gesture, when overhead
the clouds are muttering?

And how can faith intenable
come to hand salvation,
war succumbing to peace,
the heart's flutter stilled?
The ticking clock,
the ticking mind,
the clutching eye,
the tortured arm—
who is the exequatur,
my Lord or me?

beside the still waters

Shepherd, in the freighted night
the streets resound with want of you,
but in the rented rooms,
death frivols on a tousled bed.

What cabalistic sign explains
the skin unbuttoned, the bone defiled?
What swinging bulb anoints the head
and glitters on the trembling cup?

Shepherd, the shrouded gullies
muffle your step, unvoicing timbrel,
lute, and saxophone as dancers poise.
Then in the skirling mists your lamp
uncoils a shadow: comforted, I lay me down.

a young lion lurking
in the secret places

Listen, Hunter, the tears
are no more tears tonight:
look, they have dried
and fall brittle to the ground.

Spacious, the glint of skies
engulfs the solid earth:
listen, Hunter, the tears
crackle in the brush.

And still untorn
among the thickets
runs the doe:
listen with me, the tears
are like a heartbeat.

Hunter and Shepherd, hear
the doe in the rustling brake:
listen, the night is tears,
and the day a pillar of smoke.

THE SMALL GOSPEL OF PETER

Aunche es de noche

S. Juan de la Cruz

Ask me why I have come to this place,
dry-eyed, like a woman thrifty of her tears,
walking among the stones, feeling the stones
quick and cold against my feet, where
three tall stumps are silent and despoiled.

Ask me. I will not tell, now having left
wilderness behind, the lily and the rose,
the bramble in the thicket and the moist
touch of holding hands, the jungle of longing,
assuaged desire, the musketry of pleasure.

Ask me. I will not tell, now having fled
the burning city, its shriek of joy,
the neon-lit assault of laughing mouths
writhing, breaking through bubbling asphalt.

Here where three solitary stumps push upward,
barren to the reaching sky, I walk unslippered
in the ashen night, blood mingling with the dew
of sweated earth, beyond the grip of measure,
pierced by forever and worried by now.

EPILOGUE TO THE BOOK OF JOB

fac eas Domine de morte transire
ad vitam quam olim Abrahae promisisti
et semini ejus

Requiem Mass

Now Job—behold him ragged of soul
and brittle in the arteries—stood
before the opaque of his window
tense for the striking hour, uncaring
for the book of days upon his desk,
with all notations made for yesterday,
today, tomorrow, or granting it, eternity.

Job heard no requiem for glory
past or still to be, saw no sunset
as the broken light caught the dust
that hung distended in the air.
After the bells had signalled,
Job would gather up his bones
into the tentative shroud of coat
and push them to that cube of floor
and wall and ceiling he called a home.

Yet in his guarded movement through
the fever of spontaneous streets, Job
still felt the twitch of glands
raddled but still tenacious,
clutching desire, clothed in the brash
of youth—and limbering beauty
made spasms in his veins,
at his nerve-ends music.

> *The tattered song of men*
> *who miss the boat to death—*
> *the casuals of senescence—*
> *is not unlike the muddied*
> *vinegar of spoiled wine.*

And revery secondhand
a corruscated sludge
when the shining metal
has been poured into
a mold now forgotten.

Rust is the payoff,
a rusty song played
on a rusty hinge,
a rusty gate
to an empty house.

If pity knows this song
tragedy laughs; comedy
blows its putty nose.

Job can sing at evening
breaking a path to his room
through the glimmer of the city,
taking his song to his room
like mist on a platter, borne
aloft in ceremony via sharp stairs
and contemplated behind a locked door.

In darkness, before the single bulb
has cast its opulence upon a cot,
a chair, a bureau, and a length of rug,
Job shreds the tissue of his song,
retiring awkwardly to still death.

The ledger on his desk is shut
by muttering chars who see it
for obstruction to a dust-broom, not
as the meticulous record of something
grotesquely turned to nothing.
And Job is translated into bride
of Christ, laying mortality neatly
upon the bed, while spirit capers,
a Tinker Bell at ninety. . . .

The flesh lying in state upon a cot
has its own memories, parsing the past;
the spirit perched on this wretched cornice
whispers a song from Aretino.

Now street lights hang patterns
on his wall, and in his clothes
Job Thanatos sleeps and mutters,
simulates a mummy with the mange.

> *Stupid, miserable Job, where*
> *is the holiness that made you, where*
> *the choking stillness exploding into melody?*
> *Is it a gust among the towers, sighing?*
>
> *Spacious and most holy, do not say:*
> *Job, return to the dung heap.*
> *O do not say at all.*

Sleeping in sackcloth, Job
blasphemes himself before his god,
shoveling ashes till earth revolves,
and terror-drenched the sun returns.

The ledger on the desk blows open,
pavilion for dancing mice
whose waltzing feet obliterate
what Job's waning hand inscribed
by day, the secret, unuttered
tetragrammaton of maculate deception.

Sing, trumpet, quietly,
and meditate the lost of heart,
the tired in the brain,
reflective of foot.
Play, trumpet, let vibrato sing
the bursting cadenza, the tension
pocketed, felt in the hand,
caught by the rustling clarinets.

Let lip explain
what stifles in the conscience,
nerve against blood,
tears assaulting pattern.

Breathe out through twisted brass
the hesitant command to men
who live and stir and fade away.

> *Sing sadly, trumpet,*
> *in the dark night mournfully.*
> *Job will not die.*

THE TESTAMENT OF HEROD

Adonai elehenu, Adonai echad

Night prayer

By the fallen stone, cold
in the shadow of the sepulchre,
he stood among the weeping women.
Sudden light pierced the morning
and the rustle of the wind
in the olives made a moaning.

He is gone, the women said.
Begotten, betrayed, and gone.
The stone is toppled, the sepulchre
is a hovel in the cemetery.
Sighing, they left for other prayers.

Then he was alone,
tarnished in his cloak,
insolvent of the word.

Son of God, he called.
In the moment of the driven nail
when the body opened and through
human lips the lamentaton burst,
tear-washed, you were the Son of God.

When the ghost forsook the flesh,
when the dishonored body lay
solitary in the sepulchre,
you were the Son of God.

But in the dark tomb, the startled
Man stood forth, wrapped in God's hand,
recast in pain, God's chosen, God's bereft.
In death and dissolution, you were
the Son of Man, torn by the nail,
but in God's beckoning the Son of God.

By the fallen stone, cold
in the shadow of the sepulchre,
he bowed his head and let the frontlets fall.

PROLOGUE TO THE BOOK OF JESSE

If you came this way,
Taking any route, starting from anywhere,
At any time or at any season,
It would always be the same . . .

Eliot   Little Gidding

There were some men in a wilderness
lost and afraid, yet seeking for a hope:
this was then when trees were young
and skeletons a dream of bone.

They came by little steps of reason
upon an oaken door out of their tethers,
heedless of land or sun to such a place
as such frustration could conceive,
into a middle limbo, Jesse's land,
deep into time unknown, shedding despair.
And coming there, each hid delight,
nor left his reason before wisdom.

Now no man spoke
except the man called Jesse
upon whose fields they stood, the weary
Jesse who knew the tempest of the word
uncrying from a multitude of sin,
and he the welcome of his land
to these cold men of reason.

Here was the house where Jesse
moved within the orbit of his life—
from room to room, from sleep
to consciousness, thumbing the seconds.

This the men of flooded reason neared
out of the freighted wood,
pausing before this thing of wood and faith
where Jesse lived, neighbor to mountains.

It was evening now. The mountain
loomed above, but was not seen,
and overhead the stirrupped clouds
raced by the moon, fingering its light.

The wind had risen slowly, the trees
shook themselves of day, and in the smell
of night conviction of a good day coming.

—This is the harvest of my life,
said Jesse.—This house, this single world.
Now for a night and for a morning
I give it to you. I am your servant.—
And so they entered, with nightfall welcome.

Through the night the frogs sang
bleakly in the damp cistern,
and reason dozed beside a fire.

*The night is long, my comrade, the night
is very long, and the road to sleep is hard
when the heart knits and unknits
the travelled pattern of the day.*

*Th plucked guitar is sad, my comrade,
but not as sad as the wasted music
caught by earth and buried in vain.*

If the path of a shooting star is curved,
my comrade, how is the pulse's meter
quickened or stopped? If the universe
is folded within itself, what deed
of man can iron it out again?

If the sign of God is the toppled pile
or the lightning stroke or the sudden
dead, what godhead do the worms possess?

The night is very cold, my comrade, the night
is long and cold, the dismal hours
have overcome the tyranny of clocks . . .

And so to morning.

There in unclouded sun the mountain stood,
its strength in peace and violence.
And one by one the seeking men awoke,
standing in silence before the eminence
of stone, they who had known
when twilight faded between dawn and day
the startled bird grasping the sky
in fright, and emptiness and stars
gone with the plangent night.

Into the morning and the sun, out
of their rich frustration, stiff-kneed
like men in dreams, they climbed
up to the surfaces of day, heedful
of fighting heart—and no song there.

Something compels a man to move
out of the sculptured rut into
a road hardly remembered, on to a way
trodden by the wary feet of thoughts
occasional and cousin to a seldom dream:
insanity leading to mangers, mountains,
the dusty sepulchres of tortured men.

Something in man rejects the place
of birth and working, the stone-etched music,
the clatter of voices too familiar,
something caught out of time that cries:
—Let us forget the reasonable hours
of sleep and waking, the bread and wine
of comfort, the clutch of pattern;
let's turn from these colloquial habits,
placing one foot before the other.

Now in the middle stretch and looking down,
they saw the river, laced with light,
the pantomime of life below, and there
ahead the beckoning path—strophe
and antistrophe breeding discontent.

—Why are we here? the cold voice asks.
—an inconclusive mist that rises
like Lazarus and then is gone . . . ?
Why are we here, held to the leading strings
of one who scorns the commerce of our minds?
Let us descend.

—Why are we here, panting behind this man
of simple thoughts, this country philosopher,
when down below a river flows and women
genuflect between the rows of plants
or probe the earth or open mouths to sing?
Let us descend.

Then Jesse turned to them, saying:
—How wide of brow, how glib of speech,
how pawned to cruelty, how gaping in the heart.
Words become talisman, and faith remains a drab.
The living deed is man, linked to his destiny,
and no equation to a high-flown utterance.

—Having circumnavigated pride to hear me speak,
why do you flaunt your smugness? (Where
is the token of one mind, one heart, one body—
one people holding one pulse within one tissue?)

—I am Jesse, born of good from evil . . .
I am your brother, Abel before your Cain, hated
for having spied you in the bushes weeping
over pockets bulged with hoarded refuse.

—Yes, I am Jesse, a tepid man cuddling
a tepid time, climbing a hill with robots
posing as men, to say one word before I die . . .
party to a dream that man's defiance
is not a gesture in the gale, a stuttered cry,
but somber music walled against time.

—O cry at dawn because the womb is void,
and know the heat of day empty of hope.
Hoe the fresh earth and sow the anxious seed,
and water with your heart the naked patch.
And then at harvest, hide from the reaper, hide
because the earth is bare; and know that winter
comes—the ceaseless, shrill insinuation
of the cold that probes the structure of the bone,
the sepulchre of ice, the flap of wind on flesh.

—Now as we move again, up towards the peak,
measure pretense of intellect in gallon jugs,
compassion in eye-cups, hope of heaven in a dropper.
And know that reason sterilized is Dead Sea fruit,
a joke on conscience, an in-turned blade held bare.

—Before we move again, look down, minds
leashed to other minds, and see the fields
disturbed by plow, and see the people.
In their stupidity, the organism struggles,
the heart falters, mortality trembles;
yet as they stir, the universe takes heed.
Look down and see the people; be abashed.
Look down, rejecting pride, and know your seed.

Then Jesse turned to hide his sadness,
leading the lost men forward again,
and as he walked, the noonday light
swept over earth, bestowing glory
upon the mountaintop. . . .

INGEMISCO

Belabor me, O Lord,
and find my God.
Let jubilate sound,
invite the strife
of towering angels
shining in the wood.

Open the heavens,
sing the terrifying name.
O Lord who made us,
now return to night.

Beyond the tower,
beyond the fire,
negation bends
and God's tremendous sword
rings hallelujah
on the anviled souls
of surging hosts
that sanctify your blood.

Sing gloria in excelsis;
find the weeping mode.
Belabor me, O Lord,
and find my God.

KOHELETH IN CAPTIVITY

*silencio de derrota y de victoria
en que se funde al fin toda la historia
del árbol del bien y del mal . . .*

Unamuno   Cancionero

Grace at morning, the will ascendant
through porous sleep.
                              Abruptly up
from the dreams foreshortened,
on the day's gnarled branches,
the sun in riveted design
patterning the intervening hours.

Time to be up, Koheleth:
time to decode the vision of the eye,
to scan the metaphor of breath
          thwarted,
               the unclad mouth.

Time to be caught,
          gaffed and rebutted
in the maundered cadence.

          From the fumbling night
          Koheleth rises to the whip of light,
          the scourge of means, winding
          phylacteries about a waking soul.

          Standing before the mirror
          in depilatory gesture
          Koheleth is ambushed by his face.

Androgynous, empty-handed,
sulfurous in portent,
pendant and aroused,
down the street he walks
afraid to touch
the germ-ridden moment,
desire a spirochete
lazy in the lymph.

How do we yelp for you, O Lord,
shorn of all dignity,
lacking in upright flesh,
knowing that each day swallows
beginning in end, the hand
grasping time's, the exegete
plaint stuffed in the throat.

Where is the vanity,
                    the hot intrusion?
Koheleth asks.
                In the God-made plains?
In the forests?
                    Among the chortling streams?
Is the effulgence
                    in the heat-soaked seed
maturing under loam?
                    In the cold decay?

Lost, my God, lost,
                recidivist lost.
Among the stricken corn
                    the rotted hopes
are lost.
        In the winnowing fields
the blossom splits,
              the scarecrow
thumbs destiny,
            disgraces its clothes.

Lost in the pasture,
             stampeded in the glen,
the cricket's plaint
             a charge of fear.
In the brake
        the scuttling hare
careens against me
           torn by movement.
My God, Koheleth says,
              give me the ordered
terror of cities,
        the paving stones
of your rejection,
           the giant middens
packed with ashes,
         the caverns
of fornication,
          far from the fields
where clearcut
        purpose retches.

Lost, my God, lost
                        among the simpering leaves,
besieged by humming
                        bird and fox.

        The squatted moment shifts,
        the loin contracts, time
        loses its rhythm, pauses.
        Digestion, post-meridianal,
        grinds the brain.
        The cork in the bottle
        shrivels, cracks.
        Smell of vinegar
        slips to the nostrils.

Living in new houses,
we copulate in new beds,
put the press of our bottoms
on new chairs, despair
in words still mint-scratched.
But the order of our going
when the contract lapses
is old as the whisper of serpents.
In the hollow of my soul
there is no newness, only
the cold, esurient fear of Adam.

Brother, do you remember
how we loved God, and how
the sin grew from day to day?
Do you remember, Koheleth asks,
how we nourished the plant
and how the sin moved
up from the root, brother?

Now in this moment of stasis,
in this time of requiem,
of yitgadal, my head falls.
Why do you sing then?
Why do I try?

It is night, brother.
No lamps are lit
and it is dark.

LAMENT FOR DEUTERO-JEREMIAH

*und der Alte, vorsichtig, ging und verhielt das Gemuhe
einer dunkelen Kuh. Denn so war es noch nie.*

Rilke   Das Marien-Leben

At night the city spoke
in organ tones.
                    Who are you?
the vox humana asked. The quavering
treble and the bass
picked up the question: Who are *you?*

      I am my Father's son,
      who lived and wandered
      and despaired.

The solitary city did not speak
again, but there was wind.
The cadaver of stone was desolate,
the flaking dust was heavy.
Cruel and brittle, music returned.

                          I am
      my Father's son. Comfort me, Jesse,
      David, I am my Father's son.

Lost in the strangled hour,
the vox humana sighed.

II.
Among the stones the seed lay sterile,
the small babe shivered in the cellar,
the towers were shallow in the sky.
Man's track was a gutter of rain
carried seaward underground,
tasted by rats, brine on a sponge,
blood in a cold-edged glass.

III.
God came to me when I was young
and lifted up my head and spoke to me.

I am your God.
Is that enough?

God came to me when I was full of tears.
God took my hand and showed His face
and let me see His smile.

Are you my God?
I asked.
I am your God, He said.
Is that enough?

Is that enough that I have seen
Your face, and seen Your smile,
and felt Your smile upon my face?
Is that enough, my God,
now that my tears are dry?
Or should I fall upon my knees
and pray to feel Your touch?

It is enough, my God,
and not enough.
In this flat moment
it is not enough
but in the endless passion
it is enough, my God,
it is enough.

IV.
In the defiled Holy of Holies,
I stood. The dripping walls
echoed my heartbeat. Underfoot the torn
scrolls caught at my ankles,
but the note was muffled.
Only the vox humana wheezed,
intoned,
          —Why did you come back?

Rejected, acquainted with grief,
at the end day, sullen of testament,
loving God, how could I not return,
knowing whom God had touched.
When the cornet sounded, I too
could shout, I too could say,

        All is fulfilled. It is finished.
        The worm has not died. The fire
        remains unquenched. The flesh
        trembles in abhorrence.

Loving God, I held my head
and prayed.
            In the desolate
city the fires flared,
but the rains came swiftly
and I was not afraid,
for God is mindful; God is near.

UNTIL THAT TIME

Lady of Anguish:
You have seen me bend my head
upon the altar,
feeling the gold design
scratching my skin.

You have seen me take off my face
and in the nakedness
of bone
compel your fear.

Lady of Anguish:
You have watched me
strip away the flesh
and pierce my eyes.

But my demonstrations
had little meaning
and less courage.

They cast no light
upon my clandestine soul,
laying bare merely
the shadow of my love.

Lady of Anguish:
Only when I return
holding a candle
and a sword,
invested in my armor,
will you know
that my surrender
is unconditional.

...OTHER POEMS

LETTER FROM THE CITY

The azaleas have yet to bloom
and little things to push through earth.
I am too aware that with the opened
blossoms, white or scarlet, the Lord's passion
will turn upon my gut. I fear the summer
that spreads across my onetime house
like angel weed and damp disorder.
In this dry cell I open my window
but see no splash of cardinals,
no fretting squirrels on my sill.

Who will restore my blindness? Not God,
not you, holding this letter in your hand,
your eyes a-squint and wondering why I wrote.

I go no more to that street beyond the temple
where young girls lurk in the shadows,
tugging at my coat. Avoiding park benches,
I stay in my room, seven flights high,
over the brackish river, flying my buttresses.
The books you handled but never read fill
different shelves, and new poems yellow
on the bed. But the light is still unchanged,
waiting for the painter to mark it,
and beyond the light the illumination
of pestilence on my household gods.

I pray at times, misplacing the sacraments
and grasping nettles of compassion. But God
no longer answers me, and in the morning cold
there is a terrible ringing of bells.

AFTER THE SNOWFALL

They stepped out together,
cold of their ignorance,
to snow that was crisp against footfall.
The sun struck sharply at their eyes
and only a touch of wind
stippled their cheeks.

They stepped out making
a path in the void,
cutting their way silently
to the ice-buckled trees,
seeing the little wood
familiar to its sparseness,
and marked the road
still new in its whiteness.

Behind them the house
disappeared in its solitude.
The trees slipped beneath their burdens,
and the road lost all direction.
Only the sun remained their company,
but when it dropped behind the sky,
they too vanished.

GUINEVERE SPEAKS

Say to the king
I will not see him.
Why should I speak to Arthur
or he to me?
I sit here soiled by Lancelot
and by myself.
Discovery was the least of it.
And Arthur? Arthur!
Adultery is meaningless
to majesty like his.
There's more concupiscence for him
in searching for the Grail.

I touched his body—
Lancelot's, I mean—
And he touched mine.
There was no magic to it.
We might have been
bootboy and kitchen maid.
Even here in Camelot
there was no magic to it.
He was a man needful,
I was a woman lost, circling
among the knights.

There was no thought of Arthur,
not in me, not in Lancelot.
Why should there be?
Husbands are symbols too
in Camelot, or less than that.
And so we made our rut,
Lancelot and I,
tenderness clutching hunger,
parting as the skylark
burst its throat.

We wronged you, Arthur,
and you deserved it.
We wronged each other, Lancelot.
My words are spit to you—
Arthur, I mean.
I will not see him.

MUERTE DEL POETA

a Federico García Lorca

Esta noche
la muerte rasguea
la guitarra sorda,
las nubes tapan
los ojos de las estrellas.

Gritan las olas
desesperadas
y por los olivares
suena el llanto,
llanto sin consuelo.

(¿Por qué lloras, luna?)

Esta noche
sangre en la boca,
muere el poeta.
Esta noche
corre la muerte perra
por las calles.

(Luna de Sevilla,
¿Por qué te espantas?)

Esta noche
en el ruido bruto
de los fusiles
se corta la plata
voz de España.
En el polvo de la carretera
se apaga la luz de España.

No cantará más
esta boca sangrienta—
y besados de moscas
los ojos abiertos
gozan el baile
de los gusanos.

Esta noche
por el río de Sevilla,
por el Guadalquivir,
una gitana espera
y no oye el ruido.
En Madrid y en Toledo
tiemblan las ventana
del tiro.

(Ciegos corren
los caballos nocheros,
luna sevillana,
ciegas corren
tus lágrimas secas.)

Esta noche
muere el poeta
y nadie oye
el grito de España.

DIALOGUE IN A CRYPT

Tybalt speaks to Juliet:

You never spoke to me,
not really.
You never said,
"These things belong to us,
these things are true
whatever other hard commitments
commanded our allegiance."
And so we moved
each to that tired interview
of ways and means
and tears and quick regrets,
and never speaking, speaking lied,
and each in too much speaking
wrapped truth in silence.
Now, like a moment on the stage
when one small gesture
held to the breaking point
explodes in tragedy,
we focus and distort,
playing to audiences
that penetrate and soil.

Here in this crypt,
the lowered curtain
invites beginning.
But you will turn and smile,
reaching for hands
that do not twist the neck of love.
You, Juliet—I, Tybalt—
are compromised by applause.

Who makes the reckless gesture?
Will I?
Will we rip down the curtain?
Smash the proscenium?
Insult the audience
by saying that Romeo is a fool?
I do not think so.
Like actors
we are prisoners of the script,
reciting lines we never wrote
but cannot violate.

Juliet raises her head.

No. Lie where you are.
We contradict fulfillment
because I am Tybalt,
uncircumspect and quick
to draw my sword.
Weddings call for other kinds of blood,
and Romeo will come to you
a moon calf sighing.

If the auguries were right
I would deprive him of his reward
by taking you here
brutally and tenderly.
But I have killed his enemies.
I am a hostage to his fate.
I'll let him kiss those lips
and play the tragic hero.

Finally I've had my say
in the witness of these candles.
Now give him equal shrift.

*As Juliet lies back, Tybalt steps
into the shadow, and Romeo enters.*

THE COCKTAIL HOUR

Pillowed and defiled we sit;
our alcoholic wit
is sutured in this cacogenic hour,
and epitaphs come quick to flower.

Beneath the turgid light
we see the menace and the grin,
the sudden knowing, the blight
of recognition as the enemy within
sharpens a lethal word
then drops it. Was it heard?

In this tremendous room
even a whisper croaks of doom.

The decolletage
is in her knowing eyes.
Wetly through highball glass
she smiles, then shrugs and sighs.

Her glance forbids the pass,
invites the trying—
a fiddler crab advance
offering and decrying
the invitation to the dance.

This horn-rimmed frieze
now animate in epicene
striptease
finds a sexual golden mean.

A languid boy coquettes
the nonplussed male,
favors the women with a gale
of gossip, ornately sets
his Dali hand on Renoir hip.

Suddenly the trap is sprung
and through the air vents slip
vapors of dung.

AFTER PLINY

I am once more at making poems,
and someday before love knifes me
I will let you read them.

You will smile or frown
and I will say, not really meaning it,
"Paete, non dolet."

But it will hurt
with a sharp and useless cutting edge,
and I will cry when waking
on a neighbor day.

Even so, it is good
to be making poems again,
hearing their whisper of cunning
at the distress and wit of language.
It is good to make them
in the same impetuous spirit
you might have brought
to making babies.

And that too hurts
like the stab of pain not yet remembered
and felt for future times,
for of our mating
there was never more
than poems lying unwanted
on a bed.

How shrewd to let them
be forgotten there
like yesterday's newspapers,
how thoughtful of their real meaning.

Now here's another
to be forgotten too.
Non dolet, Paete,
though my boots
are filled with blood.